YES, I'M OUTRAGED!

NOW WHAT?

Preciada Azancot

Antonio Gálvez

Translated into English by Michelle Rourke

Original Title:
SÍ, ME INDIGNO ¡¿Y AHORA QUÉ?!

Edited by: Tulga3000 EDITORES, S.L. www.tulga3000.com

© 2011 Preciada Azancot and Antonio Gálvez

© 2011 of this edition Tulga3000 EDITORES, S.L.

Translated into English by Michelle Rourke.

ISBN-13: 978-1530851348

ISBN-10: 1530851343

Other books published by Tulga3000 Editores:

In English:

"The Little girl who made God laugh"
"The Universe of Safety: Making Fear Retreat"
"The Splendour of the Human Being"

In Spanish:

THE SCIENCE COLLECTION:
"El MAT: Ciencia del Dirigente del Siglo XXI"
"El Esplendor de lo Humano"
"El Dirigente Civilizador"
"El Estratega Pacificador"
"Metametodología MAT de la Innovación y de la Creación"
"Librarse de las enfermedades y de paso, aterrizar en la sensatez"

THE EMOTIONAL COLLECTION:
"El Universo de la Seguridad: Haciendo Retroceder el Temor"
"El Universo del Desarrollo: Eliminando el Dolor"
"El Universo de la Justicia: Erradicando la Ira"
"El Universo del Estatus: Conquistando el Orgullo"
"El Universo de la Pertenencia: Guardando el Amor"
"El Universo de la Plenitud: Instalándose en la Alegría"

"Sociópatas de cercanías"

STORIES:

"La niña que hacía reír a Dios"

"Cuentos de la abuela"

DIALOGUES:

"Sí, me indigno, ¡¿Y ahora qué?!"

"Un cielo de andar por casa, en cada fase de nuestra vida. Parte primera".

Both written with Antonio Gálvez.

All of them by Preciada Azancot.

In French:

"La petite fille qui faisait rire Dieu"

"Le point zéro: MAT, Métamodèlle d'Analyse Transformationnelle"

All these books can be purchased from Amazon and directly through our Web page - www.tulga3000.com - in either paperback or e-book format.

YES, I'M OUTRAGED! NOW WHAT?

To true friendship, ours.

Content

PROLOGUE

Preciada Azancot and Antonio Gálvez are inseparable friends and business partners in real life (www.mat-cachet.com). Together they have founded companies and built projects and dreams. On this occasion they have decided to write this manifesto/book together as a purely personal and token venture, joining – and attempting to transcend – that great and unstoppable movement of outrage that is shaking the world. Because they believe that it is marvellous and essential to denounce the tremendous injustices that crush humanity in this - according to them – no longer surmountable crisis, but rather collapse of one civilisation and emergence of another, which requires – in the authors' opinion – new values and institutions for designing and building a BIO-DEMOCRACY and a new philosophy of life oriented towards a BIO-HUMANISM created in the image and likeness of the human being's nature, evolved and in permanent mutation.

In the Socratic tradition, which is concomitant with the spirit of the work they do together and with the generational bridge between the genetic memory of the civilised world and the men, women and children of today, all of them in need of options, they have devised this work in the form of a dialogue between the planet Earth (written by Antonio) and the People (expressed by Preciada), the latter understood as meaning the most advanced, conscious, alive, outraged, creative, caring and truthful of the human race, irrespective of the ideology, origin, creed, race, social status or age of its members.

OUR VOICE COUNTS

- The Earth: Don't you realise how you make me worry? I've been warning you of the looming dangers for a while now and you don't pay any attention, as if you were merely hearing the rain.

In just the last few months, with the tsunami in Fukushima, the earthquakes in Haiti and Chile, the eruption of Eyjafjallajökull, the monsoon in Pakistan, the drought in Russia, the floods, storms, hurricanes and tornadoes in the US, without going back a few years to the Sumatra-Andaman earthquake, I would've thought there's more than enough evidence for you to listen to me, don't you?

You see, I'm terrified, outraged and worried for you, yes. In that precise order:

Terrified because you don't see that your civilisation is a sinking ship and that it's time for a new civilisation to emerge, much more centred on you and on me, since at the end of the day, I'll be your home for a few million years more. My fear arises and is shown to you in the form of what you call "natural disasters", which are, really, manifestations of my self, trembling for you and for me.

Outraged at how you treat yourself and at how you treat me. If you don't apply respect, sensitivity, care, justice, admiration, commitment, and joy to each other, I'd best look out, because what isn't applied inwardly, will never be applied or made to flourish outwards.

And worried, because when, as is the case now, one civilisation is collapsing, it's time to pass onto a new model of civilisation, and instead of clinging to outmoded values and institutions, to take a step forward towards more humanism, more life loving, more gratitude for the historic opportunity of change for the better. And what do I feel? I feel that none of you – well, almost none – wants to take that step forward. The movements of popular outrage against the tyrants in the Arab world and Spain's 15M are, fair enough, a step in the right of direction, but there's a lack of united sentiment, a lack of a sense of belonging to what is human. Hence my worry, because we've already been through this. And when there are no prospects and no one is proactive, the collapse of civilisations has always led to profound crises, famine and violence.

Do you understand my fear, my irritation and my concern?

- The People: As if we didn't have enough problems! I knew that with so much fear of unemployment, which already has an entire useful and educated generation idle; with so much obsessive apprehension over eruptive diseases with a moral resonance that the old guard present as apocalyptic punishments from heaven; with so much feeling of impotence in the face of bubbles created by speculating pseudo-economists that ally the interests of governors and bankers to sink the people in an increasingly incomprehensible and uncontrollable financial crisis – since, what sort of brain is capable of understanding that the same unscrupulous individuals who have generated it for the sole purpose of feeling cleverer than those who have governed before them and, in the process, to leap to the status of new millionaires, are precisely the same people who can provide ethical and just solutions to the financial and moral scandal they themselves have created? With so many parasitic and cynical politicians who no longer represent my voice nor care for my interests, instead fighting like predators in the jungle of political manoeuvring and making me argue over them against their equally unscrupulous opponents to seize my potency in exchange for my vote; with so much bad conscience – created and fed by the manipulating mass media of (dis) information – forcing me to eat in a hurry and regretfully the plastic food I manage to bring to my children's table, as if I were the one taking the bread out of the mouths of so many African children dying of hunger every minute and from so many illegal immigrants who risk their lives on life rafts seeking a job nobody else deigns to do to be able to send sustenance to their impoverished families; with so many middle-men monopolising the live forces of the fluid and natural relationship between producers and consumers and silencing my understanding of logic, making me pay huge sums for any product while they strangle producers and submerge consumers in misery, whether these middle-men be religious, social, cultural or domestic; with so much propaganda orchestrated by ideologies that have divided brothers into conflicting religions and ideological wars that in the end place in authority the same power-hungry devious individuals wearing different masks, yes,

I knew they would drive me mad, because here I am hearing voices! Supernatural voices, like Joan of Arc, or Moses at the Burning Bush! Who are you and what do you accuse me of? Who are you speaking to if only I can hear you and I feel afraid of you? Of what civilisation do you speak since there never was one, because I was always its cannon fodder and mortar for building its motorways and cathedrals? Don't you think I'm outraged enough for you to come along and defy me?

- The Earth: Dear people, no, you're not crazy. And no, I neither accuse you, nor defy you. It's me, the Earth, your planet, your home. And you can't imagine how happy it makes me to hear you answer; if you answer it's because you can hear me, and if you can hear me, it means we can talk, and if we can talk it means we can work together, and that fills me with excitement. And your outrage fills me with hope, because it's the first step towards eradicating those evils you denounce.

I ask you to trust in me, since I'm not only your home and support, but also I carry in my entrails all the human beings who have ever lived, from the most humble, to the most regal, from the most illiterate to the most illustrious, from the coarsest to the very genius. And all of them are your ancestors and there is something to be learned to do or not to do from all of them.

And for this reason, I consider myself to be not only your mother, but also your grandmother. And as your grandmother, with my clear recollection, your baggage going back thousands of years and your desire to be, I propose we form an invincible team to postulate that civilisation you dream of. Would you like that?

- **The People:** Would I like it? Not only would I like it, I yearn for it. Not only do I yearn for it, I crave it. Yes... but, there's a huge and enormous "but": look, and listen well, you who hold in your bosom the bones of my forebears, you who call yourself my grandmother. If you truly are and you truly want me to acknowledge you as such, I will introduce myself with my full credentials and you can see whether it was me you were talking to or not. I am the people. And as such, I am the human race as a whole, not a social class in bondage, fighting with concealed envy against the wealthy, no, I'm not even one more generation, sacrificed to the imbecility and short-sightedness of its predecessors, I am the entire human lineage that has not betrayed its lifelong goal and reason for being: to evolve always for the better and with peace for everyone. I am just monarchs, because some do exist today, and philanthropic bankers, and the bourgeoisie, honest estate holders and property owners, I am all the geniuses that have emerged from me and whose genetic memory is engraved in my collective conscience and who protest using my voice, I am all the humiliated hungry who are denied the dignity of what is human, I am valuable institutions that have helped to improve human beings. And I am not the cannon fodder of a new class war, or a war of religions, or ideologies, or a lamb to be fleeced for the benefit of self-seeking smart asses. I aspire to a civilisation in the image and likeness of human splendour because I declare that there hasn't been one yet. I want to make the most of the current collapse of one more non-civilisation in history, to build a BIO-CIVILISATION based on a bio-humanism in the image of the human being's organic functioning and measuring up to its genuine motivations. I am not just a green activist seeking a clear conscience by speaking in your name. So, now what do you have to say? And, ha! I was forgetting the most essential: I don't want an opportunistic association against enemies with you, but a PARTNER at the service of justice, dignity and peace. What do you say mother-grandmother? I was only born and have only evolved to become an eternal partner, not a circumstantial ally. What do you have to say to me?

- **The Earth:** Bless you – but without religious connotations, ok? And I know well who you are and recognise you, because although tremendously young for my age, you are my reason for being. I always addressed you and middle-men always came between us to "interpret" me as it suited them. I always addressed you and to date, only one in a million knew how to feel me from the depths of their soul and with all their spirit. I am speaking to you of human beings who will be very much on your mind today and who, as mere individuals, as millionth parts of you, have been capable of changing you down the centuries. Pythagoras, Socrates, Aristotle, Confucius, Laozi, Homer, Buddha, Moses, Jesus of Nazareth, Mohammed, Copernicus, Shakespeare, Galileo, da Vinci, Einstein, are just some of the few hundreds of individuals who throughout your existence have known how to perceive, albeit just a part of, that human splendour you speak of and who have spoken, not only with me, I'm not that much after all, but with the entire Universe. And for that reason, and for just that reason, a single individual is capable of changing you. That is how grateful and impressionable you are, and that is why I love you.

So, the fact that you speak to me, in a single voice, is a sign for great rejoicing, since, what won't the people, the human race as a whole, not be capable of doing if it sets its mind to it?

Me - as a PARTNER - yes, of course. As far as I'm capable, don't deceive yourself either. You can count on me to achieve your goals, not so much as earth, the Earth, a small planet of a small star in a small galaxy, that too, but as a depository of all the splendour and all the misery that has been left of you in me. And I believe I can be a good partner of yours, both pointing out the dangers that can lead to past miseries or worse, as well as indicating the opportunities that aim for and reinforce that BIO-CIVILISATION that has always been latent in you.

If you'll take me, I'm your partner!

- **The People:** And I'm yours! How nice and happy it is to feel committed, united, supported, caring and cared for on a path that, in good faith, we yearn to be total and definitive! You have just made me very happy so I'll make a date with you tomorrow to start to see, hand to tree, foot to rock and breath to venerated tombstone, and also gazing at the splendour of the stars around us, how we can start working together and forever.

... AND I DEMAND ETHICAL SAFETY

- The People: Good morning dear Partner Earth, dear mother-grandmother, due to your venerable age and given the great dame that you are, it will be a pleasure to let you go first; I propose that you start and I invite you to examine with me – I'm not sure whether you'll agree – the basis of all that is good that we'll obtain: how not to feel dread, terror, fear, locating the causes and eradicating them, so that we can then achieve the first thing a human being needs, and not just humans, to feel safe, defended and secure. What I mean is that without lasting SAFETY, we can't even stop to think, much less dream of the happiness we're all entitled to. Don't you think so, Partner? And if so, what are you afraid of?

- **The Earth:** Thank you dear Partner the People, for your deference. Our beginning couldn't be more appropriate, because without safety there is no foundation on which to build. Can you imagine if I wasn't certain that it is negentropy that sustains the Universe? Can you imagine the dread of the void, chaos, nothingness without that certainty?

I'll be very honest with you, because my age doesn't allow me to beat around the bush: in the Universe, whether we believe it or not, there is an order and that order allows, as a minute example, you and me to exist. And this isn't time for going into sterile debates between creationists and evolutionists, or the latest cosmological theories, since you, as the people, clearly perceive that there is an order of what is human, whether created or evolved – or both at the same time – that doesn't matter.

And there lies my greatest fear: that that order, that harmony, should be destroyed. And on our tiny level, this would involve altering the perfect balance of our distance from the Sun, our movement around it, our movement of rotation, the components and characteristics of our atmosphere.

And I say tiny level because we are really very small: the Milky Way has between two hundred billion and four hundred billion stars like our Sun. And the Milky Way itself is one of around forty galaxies that make up the Local Group, which in turn forms part, together with another hundred groups or clusters of galaxies, of the Virgo Supercluster, which in turn ... Anyhow, let's leave behind these dizzying figures and come back to Earth, i.e. me, as you often say!

This minuteness does not exonerate us from maintaining our equilibrium and our harmony, on the contrary, we should be delighted to obey the laws that govern and guarantee it; and the existing perfect equilibrium is already being cast doubt on by human-generated contamination and unstoppable climate change, where once the Kyoto Protocol was drafted, it turns out that the most contaminating countries hesitate to ratify it...

And if this frightens me, how much more frightened must I feel in the face of weapons of mass destruction and lethal chemical weapons? Isn't it necessary, to be truly safe, to have a way of guaranteeing peace among human beings?

These are my greatest fears, which are yours?

- **The People:** My fears? Well, I believe that I'm on the highest level of the scale of fear: the fear Little Red Riding Hood must have felt at the wolf's bedside, mistaking him for her endearing grandma. Because, is there anything more terrifying than to realise that what one most has to fear in this day and age are precisely those who should and could – if they weren't usurpers, swindlers, or charlatans – best guarantee our safety? Because it's fair enough to fear disease, death, loneliness, pain, betrayal, ignorance, yes, fair enough. At least when a disease presents itself, it doesn't do so with signs of wellbeing, of strength and vigour, or if a thief breaks into our home, he doesn't wear the mask of our son or best friend. But as is the case today, when it's precisely the democratically elected rulers, the directors of major organisations and institutions, the liberal and capitalist system and also the communist system, for which we entered two world wars and surrendered tens of millions of human lives, the dream of liberalism, the freedom to choose what job to do and how to do it, what and how to think, the right to vote, for which seas of blood were shed since slavery, the political representatives whom we entrusted to defend and protect our personal and collective interests, the legislators and judges who we appealed to trustingly to have our dignity restored, the venerated so-called wise men who facilitated our understanding of our Creator's divine intentions, yes, when it's those very people who make alliances with each other against the potency and the sanity of the People, in the name of the pathetic interests of poker players bluffing against their identical partners in crime, for the sole purpose of being the cleverest predator in the jungle, then yes, it's not enough to feel just fear, but dread. It makes one feel cornered and with no way out. It's the horror of chaos, yes, CHAOS in capital letters, of the absurd depicted by Kafka in his premonitory novels. Because, what defence can we speak of? The army, which should be our guardian angel and absolute peace professional, attacks our outraged children in front of our own windows or takes them away to foreign wars, gratuitously manufactured to serve interests that have nothing to do with dignity or justice. The resistance fighters who claim to fight for their people take shelter behind schools, hospitals and children and call it a holy war to commit suicide killing innocent people who have nothing to do with their miseries and who suffer similar misfortunes or worse, because they are disguised as patriotism and liberty, by their rulers who manufacture speculative bubbles which leave them ruined overnight, homeless and with the obligation to continue paying their ruinous mortgage out of their unemployment benefit.

Researchers are flooded with money if it's a question of inventing more weapons of mass destruction and reduced to begging in vain if it's a question of finding remedies to eradicate fatal diseases, universities erect insurmountable walls of entrance examinations to train professionals with one sole guarantee: joining the unemployment queue and unlearning the little creative intuition they had left to seek new options. Geniuses, who formerly all socialised, nowadays ignore each other and feel isolated and abandoned, because the only networks that function are for gossip and dating, and there are swarms of these. What am I afraid of, you say? You could ask me what I'm not afraid of, because then I'd only have to find one example of safety to give you. I don't even trust myself. And what's more, I confess that I've already reached the profound conviction that I'm the one I ought to fear most, because I thought I knew myself, but I don't even know who I am anymore nor what I'm worth nor what I'm good for. And if I'm to be honest with you, it's like this, hitting rock bottom, that sometimes, a flash of light, or perhaps madness, convinces me that deep down, since Socrates, not only has nothing changed, but it has even got worse. We don't know ourselves, and that's why we project what is most insecure in us and why we choose the worst believing that we're safe. I don't know. I don't know. I feel outraged, yes, but weak, without choices, without any way out. Don't you think, dear ma-grandma, that these are more than enough reasons to be terrified?

- The Earth: It's a sorry state of affairs, certainly, dear partner. And you have every reason to be terrified. Now, from that fear which you feel, let's see how we can manage to restore your strength, your options and your ways out.

You've already taken the first step: to determine where the danger lies. If the primary danger lies in you, because you don't know yourself, the second step ought to be to get to know you, to diagnose you, so that we can be certain in the knowledge of where the greatest dangers lurk in you and where your greatest virtues, which will help us to solve the dangers. Once we clarify this point, we'd have to do something similar with your rulers, with your "life forces", to see what the ideal organisation for ensuring your safety would be. Let's get down to it:

In your statement there is, I believe, a very accurate diagnosis of the current situation, from which, allowing myself to read between the lines, the following basic needs emerge for you to recover your safety:

- ⚱   A system of rule subject to criteria of ethics, a vocation of service to the people, honesty, what else?

- ⚱   A dignified legislative system, just, equitable, which makes you feel that true justice is not only divine, but also human.

- ⚱   Recognition of the wisest among you so that they can guide collective and individual progress.

- ⚱   The army – defence system – should be the guardian angel and maximum peace professional, just like you said.

- ⚱   Researchers should focus on finding remedies to eradicate fatal diseases, new sources of clean energy and everything aimed at increasing your safety and wellbeing.

- ⚱   Universities would teach how to promote their pupils' personal growth and creative capacity.

- ⚱   Geniuses should be recognised and admired during their lifetime, because, given my broad experience, they bring you pieces of Eternity, and in general, in exchange, you acknowledge them and build altars to them only when they are buried in me already and only old-fashioned academics can speak in their name. And these do so with two purposes which terrify me, while I carry them in my bosom as preferred children: first to raise their conceit above those they haven't been capable of appreciating in life and to place it over and above the silenced genius – since they believe they give him the endorsement of celebrity -, and second, to convince us that a genius is not human, that he's a half-mad creature from outer space whom we ought to fear. Whereupon they manage to make us believe that we can't imagine or create a better world, a genius world. That's what I'm definitely afraid of, partner. Because when they mortgage your creative POTENCY, all you're left with is fear, impotence, and a sense of helplessness.

What should we do to achieve this dream scenario? Excuse me dear partner for the royal "we", but you see I feel myself to be very much a partner. I know what to do, I can't do much, but I can help you think and reflect - that I can do.

Perhaps we could start by seeing what the safety system that would ensure the above would be? Having done this, we could advance resolutely to find choices and ways out for all the rest, don't you think?

- **The People:** Yes, ma-grandma, and before anything else, most dear and privileged partner. Since yes, thanks to you I'm realising that I've just made a diagnosis, as you point out, and not only of me, who is simultaneously the victim and the cause of everything else, but of the situation in general, of the causes threatening my integrity and yours. Speaking of mine, inner – because if I'm unaware of my weaknesses and confuse them with my strengths and vice versa, anyone can manipulate and deceive me – and outer – confusing the wolf with the lamb and trusting him, or worse still, believing I need his "endorsement" to believe in my own dreams, in my own certainties, in a world that is safe, developed, fair, creative, committed and flowing in peace. And yes, as my great-grandfather Socrates would say: "Know yourself!" and you will know the entire Universe - that is the key to everything.

And through this dialogue, I think, or rather know that I'll achieve it. What am I saying? That we'll achieve it! Since you Earth, no longer mother and grandmother, but also daughter and baby, will be what I most love and value, since everything in you and since the beginning of time was always patience and love, water for my thirst, and food for my hunger, and also memory of evolution, and the place that loves light above all else, in other words TRUTH, and always rotates around it. Yes, beloved partner, with you I discover that for the first time I'm agreeing to listen to you, instead of just being attentive to my morbid ruminating internal dialogues, beating myself up to see how, once more, I manage to devise the way of earning my daily bread with the sweat of my brow in a valley of tears. And it's your fear for me and of me that awakens hope in me, the potency of my imagination, of my creative power to build with you a world that is worthy of the two of us.

With regards to how to be able to guarantee maximum security on a collective level, I think it would be possible if the institutions that ought to guarantee safety, in other words eliminate the causes of fear for our integrity, were governed by a **Supreme Safety Council** elected by the Wise among the people from those who are most capable of diagnosing the level of toxicity and worth in those who could and should manage a country's administration. That Supreme Safety Council couldn't be made up of army men or politicians, or ideologists, or unconditional followers of religious dogmas, but of wise selfless philosophers and by researchers and discoverers of human functioning, by specialists in the soul and in human behaviour. To guarantee the integrity of the Nation, of Nations, just one attribute is needed which is above all suspicion: INTEGRITY, in other words, ETHICS in action.

This Supreme Safety Council would guarantee, above all else, that citizens' education focuses on self-knowledge and tolerance and delight at the other's, our brother's difference, and that way would teach us to know our weaknesses and to protect others from them, so that they become diluted in our strengths and talents. It would also direct the Army to make it the prime exponent of Peace professionals. In other words, masters at detecting any chaos, knowing how to detect and diagnose lust for power, the compulsion to control other people's conscience and to eradicate it in real time and without violence, rather with objective arguments, with a simple diagnosis of the harmfulness of those behaviours.

The Supreme Safety Council would also teach love for order, on condition that said order is of the human being's happy and innocent nature and not the institution of power relations of the most unscrupulous over the most naive.

It would also govern interior defence authorities such as the police and the Intelligence services, to make them prime guardian angels of the biological order of my members.

And, naturally, it would also govern all Public Health (including Social Security) to make prevention and the availability of medicine and everything related to the knowledge going back thousands of years or pioneer discoveries of the functioning of the human body, a multi-disciplinary science that knows how to safeguard integral health, guaranteeing it.

And, finally, it would make sure that the right to having a roof over one's head was nothing short of sacred, impossible to be the subject of speculation by the corrupt, or of blackmail to mortgage a whole life to reimburse an increasingly blind, cynical and abusive loan. It sounds like utopia, but no, it's not. It's just ethics. Will you help me, partner to state it in more, shall we say, earthly terms?

- **The Earth:** Yes, it may sound like utopia, but speaking of what it sounds like, listen, because if it's a question of earthly matters, here's the expert!

These institutions you speak of and that Supreme Safety Council could be a reality in a few years' time, let's say, one hundred, if work starts now in the right direction. Measures that I believe are realistic and applicable as of now, and which I submit for your consideration, would be:

1.- Before anything else, to institutionally promote measures for the population to know itself individually and collectively. And this should be done in the first instance through educational programmes for children and young people. In nursery schools, schools, colleges and institutes. Through a defence of childhood from the institutions, and not only from physical harm, but also from psychological abuse. In other words, we would have to advocate children's emotional security.

If every individual knows himself, and if every individual has a profound knowledge of you (People, human beings of yesterday and today) and of me (Earth, home and your collective memory), and also has the necessary emotional security, then he'll be capable of knowing what policies are suitable for your growth and what leaders you need.

2.- To promote Health and Defence policies and systems suited to the 21st century and third millennium: well scaled, managed and funded.

With regards to Defence systems, to inculcate defence from school age as a mission of peace and understanding, of coming together. And to stress it further in military academies: war is, always, a failure, and almost always, avoidable.

With regards to Health, to back a life loving Health system, devoted to love for truth, promoting a conjunction of the best from different oriental and western, ancestral and ultra-modern medicine, focused not on fighting disease but on preventing it.

3.- To promote a special defence for the safety of wise men and exceptional leaders. Not only physical safety, but also basic financial safety. This through the creation of grants, prizes and awards for the best. Once more, from the earliest age.

I believe, dear partner, that, as couldn't be otherwise, things always start from the beginning... Hence my proposal to start by working on the new generations, and re-educating present ones, since that's how the future is built, don't you think?

- **The People:** I do dear daughter! And all of it is safe and achievable if we that's what we want. And we do.

... AND I DEMAND
INTELLIGENT DEVELOPMENT!

- The People: Once safety is guaranteed, a second universal motivation of the human being arises, also present in the elements, the planets and in you dear Partner: that of using the mind, our resources, all the means available, to achieve their organisation and management in the most intelligent, compassionate, sensitive and efficient way. It's enough to look at you to realise that the fauna and flora, the seas and the rivers, the whole earth adapts to the opportunities and resources available in each time and place, and in doing so, an amazing and prodigious diversity flourishes and prospers, which is offered to us humans, not only to contemplate in awe, but to live from, to quench our thirst and hunger. If that motivation of intelligent development were met, nothing would be wasted, nothing would spoil, nothing would become ill through lack of care or oversight, nothing would suffer as a result of the insensitivity of those who are presumed to be more skilful, specialised and qualified to administrate the resources of this planet, and not only this one.

To see what is currently happening in the world, to absorb aseptic and coldly statistical information – as if it weren't a sensitive and suffering reality – about the crazy and maddening imbalance between people and between peoples who die of hunger while others fight obesity from eating junk, to know impotently how every minute children die from malnutrition and insalubrious conditions and that they will never have the opportunity to develop healthily and serenely, to observe how taxes bleed the most vulnerable to be wasted on nourishing bureaucratic administrations and parasitic luxuries, all of this, dear Partner, makes one howl in pain, suffering, sadness since only SADNESS is the correct emotion for bewailing that squandering of what is alive, sensitive, good, all that loss of opportunities, all those resources thrown to waste. Are we really so deaf that we have needed to hear the clamour of that misery, of that inequality extend to the rich world in crisis, to become aware of that monstrosity, of that degrading manner of managing and being managed? Never was the world so rich and never was there so much misery. And you know about that, you suffer from it more than anyone. And I also cry for your pain which I invite you to share with me. Tell me about it please.

- The Earth: Dear Partner, you've hit the nail on the head! And my sadness has been infinite; vaster than my oceans and my skies, than my deserts and my peaks.

For centuries - what am I saying? – I mean millennia, I have cried for you and for me. For you, because I never before could see that I'd be able to communicate with you, that I could help you find your path to splendour and plenitude and, you know? There's nothing sadder than to feel that somebody needs your help and that you can give it and that, for some reason or another, it's impossible to communicate, the basis for giving help. I cry for me because that defect of yours has manifested itself in all its horror in how you've treated me, especially lately … savage deforestations causing immense areas of desert, acid rain, the huge contamination of my/our seas and oceans, uncontrolled toxic dumping – whether nuclear or not – poor waste management, atmospheric contamination caused by means of transport and heating, indiscriminate and inefficient use of what you call "fossil fuels" – mostly coal and oil – mean that, despite my immense capacity for regeneration, my strength is failing.

And why all of this? Well, you've just phrased it extremely well: to summarise, there's a lack of sensitivity, lack of compassion, lack of care and kindness. And as I pointed out when I was speaking of my fears, if you don't apply that to yourself, as a People, to all your members, it's impossible to apply it outwards, to me.

But enough regrets. We're already communicating, we're already a team, so let's see what we can do to put an end to all our sadness. In your statement you've found the key for solving all our ills: it's a question of finding the motivation for **intelligent development**. Allow me to underline it, because it's what will help us to alleviate our ills. If we've already been capable of perceiving losses, it's time to find options and solutions that eliminate their causes, don't you think?

What can you come up with that we should do?

- **The People:** Beautiful partner, many solutions came out of me in the course of those millennia you speak of, but intelligent solutions, never. Intelligence, kindness, care, sensitivity, honest communication between equals, understanding the other person's hurt and pain, not just putting oneself in the other person's shoes, yes, all that, which is simply the manifestation of the capacity to feel the loss of something alive and good, in other words true sadness, is in fact the only non-contaminating fuel to set the rational and intelligent mind in motion. The mental clarity that emerges from its confusion, its disorientation, in short. In other words, the very essence of Civilisation, of what is not barbaric, because it is not provisional, not circumstantial. And I say, now that we've started reasoning, I say, wouldn't it be that everything comes Just in time as the English speaking peoples who form part of me say? Might it be that everything comes at the exact right time and that there never could have been a Civilisation in capital letters, at least not the start of it on this earth, before I could hear your voice, before you and I could communicate?

And if before I couldn't hear your voice, it's because before today I hadn't been able to mature, I hadn't yet been able to become an adult and to understand the minimum understandable: we can only save ourselves together, caring for each other and never against each other. We wish to save ourselves together, precisely because, today more than ever, everything encourages us to find more scapegoats, more culprits outside, to choose more selfishness, more avarice and more lack of care, in other words anti-compassion. In other words and stated – I suppose – more intelligently: the time for self-pity is fortunately over. The time of Noah's Ark and the Apocalypse has already passed; the time of the war between races, religions, classes, genders, and generations has already been and gone. All that is over, and that's called being mature.

Perhaps, and I hope to have guessed right by calling you baby, my baby, you were also very young to raise your voice loud and clear enough for me to have heard you. I don't hear ultrasound, or perhaps I do now. You know what? I always dreamed that before I decided to move for real, the time of Noah's Ark would end, which I call "No-ah!" (in other words the ark of those who had to be accountable for others' blame and obey rigid commandments) and the time would come when the entire planet was that Ark, which I call " Yes-ah!" (in other words the time for building hand in hand a world of understanding and sensitive and caring communication). I hear strange rumblings coming from you, are you laughing? Or crying?

- **The Earth:** I'm laughing, sweet partner. I'm laughing with joy, because when the fresh intelligence of your being flows, nothing seems unachievable, everything seems possible, and also clear, like the most limpid of waters! And I share your intuition: it's now that the time has come for us to resolve what, each for their own part, believed impossible.

And now we're at it, I allow myself to outline the type of actions that spring to mind to set *our intelligent development* in motion:

♥ A first step is for you to assume and recover all the parts of you that were healthy and beautiful and that got lost along the way. I'm talking about recovering and incorporating, updating them, past eras and concepts of splendour, such as Greek philosophy and the Renaissance in the West, and in the East the Ming dynasty in the Buddhist world, the Umayyad dynasty in the Muslim world, and of equal or greater importance, to recover and incorporate, updating them, the thoughts of key personalities in your history, some of which I already mentioned when we were discussing safety.

♥ A second step would be to place the initiative for development in people and society, replacing middle-men and public authorities with valid and effective functional coordinators.

♥ Knowing how to eliminate the causes of sadness, present or future, means knowing how to distinguish, in each individual, in each situation, in each opportunity, what is alive, what is diseased and what is dead. And here education and social means of communication play a very important part, as they must serve to educate you in the knowledge of yourself and to allow the development of the individual and collective potential, and not to confuse, invade, shoot down and spit out half truths.

♥ And we would have to think about designing the ideal body or entity that would ensure development, not only of the currently fashionable "sustainable" type, but also life loving and intelligent. And of course, with the unmovable base of having safety guaranteed, since otherwise, we would be building on feet of clay, as has been the case on other occasions. This body would look after education on all levels, communication, transport and social and economic development.

What does this sound like, dear partner?

- The People: It sounds like intelligent clarity, and like compassion for me of the good kind: with passion! And this requires loving the way you do: passionately and putting one's life at the service of caring for what is loved. In this, I believe, lies the solution, the key, the secret recipe for development that we must learn from you. It's this attitude, this intention, this attentive honesty that will be the key to any success.

Because there have been millions of drafts of institutions based on education, on mass media, on good intentions, projects, reforms, attempts, but I believe that just as it's unavoidable to make development rest on guaranteed and firmly ethical safety, we should make it clear that the philosophy that should guide us all could be based on a single idea: *there is no clear intelligence unless it comes from the heart, and there is no passionate love unless it is based on reason.* Since intelligence without heart makes for bureaucrats and human machines, and loving passion without reason only self-destructs leaving the object of love feeling full of guilt and insecure: it weakens it; it doesn't make it flourish.

Having said this and on this basis, yes, I fully agree with you. If we hadn't started by killing, by individually allowing the best in us to extinguish itself, we would never have allowed nor considered it inevitable to spoil or neglect something outside. I believe that Creation, or the result of Evolution, little does the order of these things matter, whether of the elements, plants, animals or men, is perfect and encloses splendours and treasures yet to be discovered but all governed by objective and scientifically provable laws. If we don't know what our true hidden talents and our real personal vocation are, based on our existential passion, we cannot bring a life loving and wholesome development out of ourselves. And that refers us back to what we already said about self-knowledge.

Instead of multiplying pathetic nationalisms and localisms that rankle around defensively preserving the vestiges of local anachronistic cultures, wouldn't it be better to back a universal identity and a universal language that would serve to extract from each human being his differential talents and to motivate him to display them confidently, to put them at the service of his group, which is also the entire human race?

With regards to the second and third point, you already expressed it so perfectly that I can only agree, gratefully. And enthusiastically.

With regards to the institution that would govern development in each country, each continent and each group of continents, if that Supreme Safety Council existed formed precisely by people who were FREE from any ideology or personal interest and capable of diagnosing and proposing the best, the most talented, those with the best vocation of loving service, instead of ministries we would have something like companies and cooperatives of managers of the major areas of national, transnational and international interest. On condition that a sovereign body that truly represented the live people as a whole were the guardian, and if appropriate, attorney, of the honest coordinators and managers that have been entrusted to manage properly the development of everything that is alive and valid and that peoples the earth. Shall we provisionally name it the MANAGING TEAM? And there would be many coordinating bodies between continents and we would all be devoted to eradicating the causes of under-development, whether intellectual, financial, moral or educational.

We are in an age of networks, and we would have to place them truly at the service of caring and multi-disciplinary human intelligence.

- **The Earth:** Have you noticed? I'm much calmer listening to you. If that's how we were to advance, the sky would always be deep blue.

AND I DEMAND IMPARTIAL JUSTICE!

- **The Earth:** And now we've got the ball rolling, once safety is assured and development is guaranteed, is it time for a third universal motivation of the human being? I'm sure that's the case, but I suspect it's not in me... Since I do have intuition, and since I hold within me the memory of millions of people who were the victims of injustice, I believe that now we should look at how to eradicate injustice from this World, am I right? I have a feeling I'm right, so without waiting for your confirmation, I'll enter the ring!

Many human beings have been and are the victims of injustice, manipulation and aggression. I've also been the victim of countless attacks as we've been seeing. However, I don't have the energy capable of dealing with these attacks, the capacity because, don't you think that if I did, I wouldn't have tried and wouldn't be trying to react against so much aggression towards me? I wish...

What comes to me from the millions of human beings buried in me is that for justice to exist a precious energy is required which is RAGE, understood as the capacity, precisely, to react against injustice, manipulation, lies and aggressions. And you do have that, and you share it with the animals, which are also capable of reacting against everything harmful.

I would love it if, after our conversations, I could, at least, dream of a World of justice in which I would never miss not feeling rage, because I wouldn't need it! And in which you used it positively, in other words, by creating more justice every time, wouldn't that be rather fine?

Injustice is everywhere we look today, starting with the unorthodox methods of Guantánamo, followed, in that same region, by populist dictatorships and continuing with the abuse of power in all the countries of the world by the authorities in control, with attacks on ethnic or religious minorities, with child abuse and gender abuse, with violence, with mafias, with the buying of favours, with turning a blind eye on disgraceful conduct, with having, in any country of the world, different standards depending on the accused. Also, and most scandalously, injustices are committed against the weakest, the most defenceless, the neediest.

Dear partner, how do you think injustice could be eradicated from the World? And how could we achieve this without victims? And what would a fair World be like? And how could we inspire unanimity and eradicate the word "enemy"?

Forgive me for so many questions, but you see this issue particularly worries me, and only you can guarantee the peace we both need, and I trust you blindly.

- **The People:** Thank Goodness you say – and I always believe you – that you don't feel rage! What a master you are already by just bearing in your breast, in your afflicted memory, so many injustices suffered by humanity! Now I definitely see you again as my beloved baby to be cared for and defended against your enemies, me to begin with. And I ask you to forgive me, genuinely ashamed at so much generosity, so much temperance. Yes, I repent and I'm fully prepared to eradicate from within me those behaviours that are always, rash, primary, and immature, since evil always begins with human stupidity and then meets one's own ego – insensitive and paranoid always – which to back comfortably, and that is called conceit, and aggravating the wrong behaviour, one reaches narcissism and from there onwards it's just one step to becoming a dictator and then a predator. This is walking in the opposite direction to the human biological path.

And yes, you pronounced a marvellous word, a key word where real justice is concerned: UNANIMITY. Unanimity based on good will, on the presumption of innocence, on the unswerving desire to suppress the word "enemy" in order to replace it with "involved interlocutor", by "team" and in the end, by "partner".

Since we are all one and every particle of our being holds within it the entire Universe, and not just on a conceptual level, but in reality, made flesh.

It is not enough to say "Not that way!" and to denounce injustices or lies. We always have to add "This way!" which offers valid alternatives that raise the benchmark between two interlocutors, offering them higher values to place them both on a level where hate is no longer par for the course, in other words, that places them on a level where both have more and better CULTURE. Because true debate is the mother of culture, the impossibility of single thought and the subjugation of those in conditions of numerical inferiority. Because we're in a right mess if we believe that the numerical majority is right! If this were the case, nothing would ever move, much less transform.

And yes, also. I say loud and clear: "I'm outraged, now what?" because if I'm outraged it's my obligation to find how to say "This way!" for you and for me. And because I am truly outraged I seek solutions instead of destructive criticism.

You see? I understand that this historical moment we are living, doesn't correspond – as strategists and official leaders are still claiming – to a crisis, but to the collapse of a civilisation and the emergence of another. And do you know how I understood it? Well, quite easily: when, as in all the decadent civilisations that have preceded us, politicians and even intellectuals and academics, instead of seeking options and solutions all started searching for scapegoats and fighting between each other like a circus sport. And since dishonesty is what rules in that situation, along with the desire to preserve a civilisation that no longer has anything to offer, the following become fashionable and in this order: a couldn't care less attitude among parents, cynicism among youth, escapism among the elderly, nihilism among thinkers, and sophism among the people's representatives. Fortunately, young people had children and these are no longer consumerist and indifferent. And they seek symbolic grandparents to guide and support them. This is another generational bridge, which is very fashionable for finding level-headed solutions for everyone.

Politicians no longer represent us, because they are the bureaucrats of political parties that merely pursue power for themselves, but in a sort of symbiotic see-saw of allied pseudo-enemies that alternate enough to blame each other for the disasters that take place, and all of this at a time when all ideologies are surplus to requirements and have collapsed, materialistic communism as well as predatory liberalism. But politicians and middle-men are not the enemy. Individually I'm sure that there are many and very good politicians and middle-men, who are human beings with a vocation to serve and who could be recycled outside of their political parties. And who surely feel stupid because they are forced to recite party slogans or catchphrases for commercial interests which are no longer even that and which make them feel like fraudsters and mobsters too.

I believe that we're in a period of history in which human beings want to govern their destiny directly. And for that reason, nothing better to suggest than a PEOPLE'S CHAMBER elected from members of professional colleges, craft guilds, district communities, representatives of religious and ethnic minorities, and not just to appear at local and popular meetings – that too – but to govern destinies and culture on a NATIONAL level, to negotiate values, to control, reward and penalise the actions of managers and even members of the National Safety Council and the National Management Team if they deviate from their vocation of social peace professionals and intelligent and honest managers, respectively. And those representatives ought to be paid, yes, but part-time, and to have the obligation to continue working at what they do, living immersed in the guild, neighbourhood, community they represent. It's not a question of replacing power professionals for union bureaucrats. At the same time, trade unions are also anachronistic, and based on a class enemy ideology.

In summary, it's not possible to create culture, to choose better values, to create a valid and irreplaceable leadership because it is based on each person's talent and vocation, and to see and treat the other person as an opponent at the same time. The other is always your potential partner. Always. And the more opposite we seem, the more complementary we are. But for that we need to wish wholeheartedly to build a Bio-Humanism, in the image of the human being and the earth on which he lives.

Does it sound like utopia again? I fear that in today's cacophony, yes! But I know that it's not, it's not utopia, but what necessarily lies ahead, because I wish it so, and because you yearn for it, and because it is fair.

And the best evidence that it isn't utopian is by going back to what you, beloved Partner, pointed out in passing: animals do feel rage, and they aspire to build a fairer society, they have values, leadership and culture. You who have buried in your bosom so many dead and slaughtered animals, you who hold in your memory, the movements, free and splendorous corporality of those animals, you who feed all live animals right now - at least those species we haven't allowed to become extinct, which are increasingly less - don't you think we should first awaken our vitality, our animal culture, and be, to begin with, worthy of them before aspiring to reign over them?

- The Earth: Dear partner, of course I do! If you're capable of creating and offering safety, if you're capable of what we've called intelligent development but you're not capable of using your rage to protest against lies and invasions and creating more justice, you are not even at animal level, much less human. And to remain at the level of a potato, best call it a day, don't you think? Joking aside, the first thing we need to do is to detect what isn't right and I believe that you've detected perfectly what isn't right about the current situation. And you're proposing how society should be organised to be represented by a People's Chamber. This seems splendid to me, but before we go on, and returning to your suggestion about analysing your animal features, it is fundamental that you perceive the reality in which you live, that you perceive things as they are here and now, that you cure and remove concepts and ideas that were valid before, but that are now obsolete.

And it is also fundamental that you look after your health and physical wellbeing, promoting sport and a healthy lifestyle. The famous "mens sana in corpore sano" from the Roman poet Juvenal, also ought to be interpreted as meaning that in a healthy body, rage is authentic and healthy and capable of perceiving reality as it is.

From there onwards, from unanimity in the perception of things and situations, unanimity can be sought in the search for new values that lead to a new culture, which, alive and alert, ensures that nothing places "glass ceilings" or hindrances on more advanced, more pioneering, individuals and groups.

In parallel, you need to find the way to lay down the bases for real universal justice, including of course the judicial and penitentiary system, which currently remain medieval.

And your idea of the People's Chamber seems fantastic to me. That smells of real democracy. Although for many the word People may sound left-wing or populist, we've already made clear at the beginning of this dialogue what we mean by People, so being your Chamber, it can't be more democratic.

So, how to advance with these issues? Well I believe that by making proposals, manifestos, submitting proposals and programmes for debate and searching for consensus, certainly, then moving into action, don't you think?

On this point I have a question that I'm sure you can clarify: How can we do things so that those among you who don't want to see reality as it is, moreover, those who don't want to change things because they are comfortable or benefitting, back your proposals?

- The People: I will start, dear partner, by replying to your last question, obviously the hardest, regarding unanimity. It's not a question of stifling the action, the protest, the beautiful movement of the Outraged that started out in France with a short manifesto from a grandfather who reminded us of the values of the resistance under General De Gaulle, spread to Arab countries dominated by dictators, and reached Spain in a much more modern, contemporary way and will spread, I'll spread it, worldwide. It's not a question of seeking the endorsement of the worst, who are not only not the People as we understand it today – in other words as what it really is: the community of those who yearn for authentic justice and who do not have invasive and harmful vested interests to defend – nor is it a question of waiting for the parasites who live off institutionalised injustice agreeing to listen to the voice of a new civilisation based on bio-humanism.

It's a question of continuing to advance, debating and acting, in peace and encouraging consensus and dialogue, more each day, more each hour. As the trumpets of Jericho did in their day. By the way, if you agree, we'll leave to one side these basic outlines that must govern a new civilisation for our next debate, because I believe that where that is concerned, it's not so much a question of rage and justice, but of pride and transformation, the human being's only and exclusive dimension, in other words the privilege and responsibility of man and woman on this earth.

Here I refer to what is distinctive in us as animals, to the SOCIAL animal in us. And I say this in admiring and superlative terms, not in a paternalistic tone.

Animals have leadership and base it on real strength and responsibility. If, as I already suggested, we base the leadership of each child, each adult and each elderly person on their real talent, the only thing that makes them unique and irreplaceable, and on their authentic vocation, we'll have a fair, cultured, and happy society. There are already ways of detecting those individual and differential values in each person. That need is for self-knowledge, we already saw it when we discussed safety. Since anyone who aspires to lead others without being able to lead their own lives towards the best in themselves, can only be a bitter corporate climber and a social castrator. They would be less than an animal.

Animals have culture, they have values and they follow them to the letter. They do not start flattering or fearing the leaders of other species who follow anti-values like those we have already denounced during our discourse on safety, development and this phase of justice. Each guild, each sector of activity, each gender, each generation, each neighbourhood association, each minority, must have a voice and a vote in that People's Chamber. And discard middle-men who do not represent anything other than clots in the flow of communication, placing obstacles in the way of problem solving.

The values that must rule society are above all A NATURAL RIGHT, UPDATED, BIOLOGICAL, CERTAIN, based on new definitions and on the evidence of a genuine scale of motivations innate to the human being.

This scale is and universally: first safety defined as we did, in other words as suppressing threats to integrity and rejecting chaos and the denial of the human being's vocation for peace and happiness. Then comes the motivation for development, as we said, in other words, sensitivity to losses and the search for solutions of intelligent development. Then comes justice, as we are looking at now, in other words the capacity to denounce, here and now, lies, aggressions and manipulations and to search for values based on the talented and vocational leadership of the best and most qualified, since only they can raise the ceiling in the measure of what is possible at each moment. Then something marvellous opens up which is inherent to the human being, the possibility of building a transforming civilisation, through creation, scientific discovery and art. Next we move on to real belonging, in other words to love for the best in us and in the best, to commitment towards each and every individual's existential passion. And finally we can make way for the last and most important item, plenitude, in other words the cult of truth and peace, the only guarantors of the human being's and your vocation for happiness, in other words of the entire Universe created and evolving.

And we must admit once and for all and denounce, the social and philosophical lie on which the human race, in other words, I, the People, have been raised and obliged to transmit to our children: I refer to that same biological scale of motivation, but inverted, upside down. In other words, the joy of winning an arm-wrestle against an opponent, then sectarian love that can be bought for those who think similarly and who form part of our team of opponents, then the fight for power over those whom we, allegedly, love, then the imposition of false leaders who serve to freeze emerging living forces, then insensitivity against the pain we cause, and finally an endemic insecurity, which we consider the best weapon for manipulation and social subjugation, which stirs the ghost of exclusion, misery, disease and death for those who do not share those anti-values and that predatory vision of themselves which we have imposed on others and on ourselves.

Unless we discard that false and deceitful, abusive, blackmailing, vision of the human being and his profound, innate, biological motivations, everything, absolutely everything that we aim to build will be like Sisyphus's rock, it will only roll downhill at the last minute and leave us feeling weaker and more disoriented. Those are the "lifelong anti-values" that we must set right, redefine and replace with those that do govern our healthy body, our real body, and consequently our sense of justice, our social sense, in short.

Forgive me, partner, for insisting so much on the philosophical, basic concepts under this heading, but if we speak of a new civilisation, that's where we must begin, wouldn't you say?

- **The Earth:** Dear partner, how could it be otherwise? Without that, we wouldn't have any foundations to build on.

I love your description of the biological scale of motivation and how it works when inverted. Just like that. Between us, I must say that it sounds so natural and you present it in such a simple concise manner, that it must be true! On top of making me feel happy and safe, imagining that you will work according to that scale of motivation, my love for you grows and that same sequence resonates with me because I always felt that I had an ordered sequence in me: as the Earth, I have only three of the six dimensions you mention and the sequence is as follows: I start with love, commitment, offering all the beings who inhabit me – plants, animals and human beings – a safe space in which to develop and be, and from there I move on to the happiness of knowing that I am infinitely small in a perfect Universe, an irreplaceable and dispensable, an infinitesimal part of the everything that at the same time contains it. And from there the safety that it gives me to reject chaos, since it is sufficient to see my seas and my mountains, my valleys and my skies to know that I am safe and harmonious. My safety is also shaken when, as I told you at the beginning of our conversation, there is a threat to love and joy. Then I'm afraid. Afraid for you and of you. And if you look at it closely, if you work in the biological sequence you describe to me, you work generating negentropy and not only adding yourself to my sequence, but multiplying it. Isn't that beautiful, dear partner?

- The People: For sure, my pure and innocent baby! You are a generator of that negentropy that nourishes everything good, dilutes chaos and sustains me. Please forgive me for having lived like an irresponsible foetus leaving you to sustain me while I, joyfully, convinced by the academics studying the functioning of human being that I had only three dimensions, in the image and likeness of the four elements, like the cliché adopted by the ancient Greeks made us believe. To discover that the human being has six dimensions has required leaving childhood behind and deciding to think for myself.

...AND I DEMAND INSTITUTIONALISED DIGNITY!

- The Earth: You are more than forgiven, dear partner, because you ask for my forgiveness from the bottom of your heart, now you have realised your mistakes and are on the path to eradicating and correcting them. THAT WAY, YES!

And speaking of building, isn't it now time to tackle a fourth topic, to see how it would be possible to build a transforming civilisation, through creation, scientific discovery and art? You were telling me that it's a question of pride and transformation, and that that's a purely human dimension. I corroborate that, since only in you have I seen that wonder, and I bear the memory of indelible, dazzling creations, which have represented a quantum leap for the human being, a leap in terms of perceiving pieces of eternity.

And I believe that it is now, as we begin to glimpse that justice is possible, that we can speak about this.

From what I can understand, that pride and that transformation are recognisable when, after hundreds of years, thousands of years, the creations continue to be contemporary, continue to be alive, continue referring you to something eternal, and continue to move you. Sticking to the world of art, aren't Mozart, Van Gogh, el Greco, Bach, Shakespeare, Cervantes, Monet, Cézanne, Rodin, to mention just a few examples, terribly contemporary for you? Don't you have the feeling that they have always been there and always will be? That without them and their works, life wouldn't be the same? With my capacity for amazement, I never fail to give thanks for the enjoyment that all of them provide for you and for me.

And herein lies a question – or rather several – that I've always wanted to ask you and cannot resist putting to you now: why, save for a few exceptions, were these people never acknowledged in life? Why have you needed me to bury them in my bosom before recognising them? Why, almost since you exist, have you thought that these people and their creations were inspired by the gods, by the whimsical wand that "illuminated" the few, leaving the rest of the world in the dark? Why, in most cases, do you associate the genius, which is how you refer to those people, with madness? Why, at the end of the day, can't all those human beings who give you life, access that marvellous dimension?

I'm not ashamed by my boldness because my intuition tells me that through answering these questions, dear partner, you'll find the way of building the civilisation that you and I dream of, since in that one, truly for real, I would feel safe.

- **The People:** With every reason you would feel safe, dear partner. And more so would I. To give you a concise generic answer to all those questions you raise, I could say – modestly I believe – that it would be a question of EVOLUTION. Yes, the great secret where pride is concerned is to define it, first and foremost, in active and passive terms. And I smile at you, because just as we have outlined the definition of authentic rage with its ideal way of expressing itself in terms of "Not that way, this way!" we will do the same now: authentic pride has nothing to do with its monstrous deformities such as arrogance, egomania, and narcissism. That is just anti-pride. Pride is above all dignity, it's measuring up to EVOLUTION and the differential dimension that every human being possesses structurally, innately, over everything else, whether elements, plants or animals. And I don't see why it couldn't be that someday in the near future, scientists will prove that everything began with an incipient element that started evolving until it became one of the four elements, which in turn, evolved until it became a plant, then an animal and then a human being. And that in turn, the human being will continue to evolve, acquiring further dimensions that allow him to teleport, mutate once again and to live in two places or historical periods at the same time. Everything that seemed like science fiction has turned out to be just an imagination of what the future would be like. To imagine is the function of human pride. This evolutionist approach can only be complemented with the creationist concept of a perfect Creation governed by perfect laws. A Creation that is so perfect that when left alone with itself, it always aims for more, right?

So it was that in Antiquity, the gods were attributed the "choice" of somebody deserving to inspire to reveal to their surroundings, in a creative rapture of mystic resonance and through their works, those pieces of perfection, of Eternity with which to delight mortals. It was the infancy of civilisation. True. But at least they recognised in the greatness of the work the creative genius, the civiliser of human thinking (such as Socrates, Plato or Aristotle) a supreme STATUS. And while they lived. Before, until the last century, geniuses all knew each other, encouraging and admiring each other – since admiration for what is great is the primary and essential expression of pride -. And kings and patrons considered it fair and awarding of status for themselves, to maintain them in their courts, fighting to attract and take care of major artists and discoverers. That's what's called being civilised.

But nowadays geniuses ignore each other, they believe they're lonely and in exile, while networks devoted to all manner of marginalities and futilities proliferate. Middle-men, be they called gallery owners, museums, academies, universities, magazines, non-creative art critics, mass media, consecrated networks, have appointed themselves authorities at detecting, recognising and consecrating the greats. Except that they manufacture those alleged "greats" in marketing factories, in their own image and likeness.

They forget an essential truth: only a genius is capable of recognising and consecrating another genius. And he wants and needs him alive, happy, acknowledged, admired, and valued in short. Because he sees him for what he really is: a beacon and a mirror of the talent and genius that sleeps, anaesthetised for now, inside every human being, in his distinguishing talent that I was advocating for the leadership of the future – here I'm not even mentioning the vocation, which is much higher, motivating and important than the talent and that we'll see further on.

If envy against what is good, high and beautiful, if the creative stature of a pygmy, if the desire for power and control that gives or withdraws approval of the titan, dominate – as is the case today among the middle-men who fade us out – they need the great to be dead, considered crazy, marginal invalid dreamers. And they do this to be free to speak in their name, to adorn themselves with the status usurped from them, to enrich themselves by speculating and inflating the prices for their works, scorned in their lifetime, to make me, the People, evolved and creative, feel that I was only born to obey and to fake ecstasy at what they choose in my name. And to make me fear being a creator, a transformer, a genius, an advanced being, because choosing that path – I am told – is social and existential suicide. And that outrages me. It outrages me precisely because what defines pride, its very definition is the innate capacity to affirm dignity, to admire what surpasses us, to create, to grow and to make grow.

That way those middle-men aim to frighten me away from my most marvellous dimension and potency. And that makes me supremely outraged.

All I ask of you, dear partner, is to please remember and tell me: among all the human beings buried in your bosom, to whom do we owe the major civilising leaps in history? To middle-men hungry for control, chaos and darkness or to great innovators, thinkers, discoverers and artists, all of them exponents of the human being's only differential quality: his capacity to transform the world into a more beautiful, more creative and more civilised place? Please, dear partner, I need to refresh, rejuvenate, and enlighten my memory.

- The Earth: My admired Partner, what a magnificent account! With that clarity, we can solve this with one stroke of the pen. And with the first stroke, we should put in their rightful place all those who, as you rightly say, sit on the shoulders of the greats, believing themselves superior for it even though they're just bothersome flies. Because so much stupidity causes me shame and fear.

Regarding your question, it's more than clear! It is, and always has been, the great innovators, thinkers, discoverers and artists who have made it possible for you to make great civilising leaps. And always, in an extremely generous manner.

And now, since I know you like my own child, allow me to reflect on your way of being, which may shed some light on how to approach this subject and set things straight: since your origins as a People, with those six human dimensions we have concluded you have, there are three that I've always seen as somewhat imbalanced: the dimension of development and sadness has always been greater than the other five. This means that on many occasions you miss the past, you regret that which could have been and was not, you feel disoriented and confused about your path, you believe that although technologically you have progressed, deep down something happens similar to Sisyphus, forced to push a large rock to the top of a mountain, with it rolling down every time he was about to reach the peak, and having to start all over again. And that is how you feel with regards to your philosophical, moral, ethical and spiritual progress, am I right?

In respect of the dimension we're now discussing, that of status and pride, it would seem, from the outside, to be a dimension that you have disconnected, except in rare an honourable cases among those exceptional beings that we've referred to as geniuses, and replaced in most cases by envy, or by amputating acts against what is great, what stands out above the average. This is fully in vogue today, don't you think?

And to conclude, regarding the main unquestionable dimension of this dialogue, the one of rage, justice and culture, I have a feeling that it's a dimension that down the centuries and millennia has been forbidden to you, which you have felt as something dangerous and destructive that ought to be feared. And of course, how could it be otherwise when in general you've felt rage when you should have felt pride, resulting in envy? But that, dear friend, should not prevent you, once you have realised that authentic rage is "Not that way... this way!", and that envy is nothing other than false rage instead of true pride, from giving that dimension its rightful place.

Why am I telling you all this? Well, because if you identify yourself with how I've described you, you can imagine that by reducing the dimension of sadness to its correct measure, you'll recover and reconnect your creative dimension, that of true status and pride, and after that you'll be able to remove the prohibition of your rage and to recover your vocation as a creator of culture, as a civiliser, which is what truly satisfies you and gives meaning to your life.

I may venture, since I know you well, that the dimension of status and pride, once recovered, will be your talent, and greatest source of genius, the one in which you'll display all your creative splendour. And there's a reason why it's the dimension that distinguishes you from all else, am I right? If you feel the same way, SHALL WE EVOLVE TOGETHER, MY DEAR?

- **The People:** Done, partner, let's evolve together! And yes, in my childhood and in my adolescence, which finished as soon as I was able to hear your voice, I did function like that, like that Sisyphus, and here I am. But today, and after expressing my outrage – partially yet, I must add smiling cheekily – I can already say that I assume myself as a young person and perhaps, in some aspects, even an adult. And yes, I've no doubt that the self-consecrated authorities, middle-men of all types, will no longer hide my virtual and real POTENCY. Because that's what it's about: recovering my potency in the face of those who only aspire to mortgage it from me to acquire the opposite of potency: power, control over my life, my destiny.

Yes, I was too much of a sad and resigned fatalist, you're totally right. And it's not to justify that past defeatism of mine, but you will agree than on a planet where in the West I'm damned with expulsion from paradise as the punishment for an alleged original sin, condemning me to earn my bread with the sweat of my brow while my wife gives birth to our children in pain, and in the East I'm silenced with the cult to the elders and automatic obedience to established authority, you'll agree I didn't have it easy.

But, joking aside, yes, the basis of my leadership over myself – in other words to become a leader of my own destiny – is the consecration of creative, transforming, discovering pride, and the demand that it be honoured as it deserves. Without this, I'll always be treading on quicksand. So I'm going to imagine, represent and declare what type of measures would guarantee that the best creators, discoverers and civilisers protect and shed light on the path of the less advanced. Let's try and see what this tastes like, dear partner:

In every country I would track down the major creators, discoverers, and geniuses and would form a COLLEGE OF CREATORS, a sort of institutional authority for detecting live potential, consecrating what is great and creating training programs to manage the talents of every human being, to educate them in refinement and sensitivity towards what is great and elevated. And I would make them be selected by other internationally recognised masters. Candidates would present themselves at their own initiative, without anyone's endorsement, irrespective of age, nationality, colour, gender or creed, since to have them is an honour and prestigious for the Nation that deserves and knows how to value, pamper and care for them. I wouldn't allow old-fashioned middle-men to choose them. This College of innovative Creators would have consultative powers, since they don't like to compete nor exercise power, but it would be compulsory to publish their recommendations and to publicise their edicts and to allow them free expression in all mass media. What would their functions be?

Firstly, as I already pointed out, to discover and obey the laws governing the way people function, detecting their distinguishing vocations and talents and sustaining their personal leadership on those strong points, those levers that catapult us towards the peak of our potency. And starting with children. So that nobody can twist them or invite them towards resignation. The dream scenario, the ideal, would be to discover those perfect laws that could already establish those talents and vocations in the foetal stage, meaning that from the moment of gestation and first infancy, they were encouraged first in the family, and then at school.

In second place would be the creation of programmes for detecting creative and innovative talents and to consecrate them without making them pass those pathetic obligatory exams and academic tests, since in those cases, the examiners are in general far below the level of the examined pupils. I would also penalise envy, which ought to give rise to shame and mockery in the event of somebody succumbing to that aberration.

In the third place, I would ask that College to create one or several methodologies to promote and facilitate JUMPING SCALES, in other words: helping someone to leap from being an imaginative individual to the following scale and become creative, and from that scale, to be able to jump to the scale of creator, then genius, then civiliser, then leaping to becoming a pacifier, and then a Partner of Creation in Evolution. The world would be marvellous, and its order outstanding beauty and harmony. Don't you think?

In the fourth place, I would investigate the order of beauty in itself, in other words, the Hierarchy of existential priorities and values that guarantee the success of the world's peaceful and enjoyable transformation. And I believe I have an idea of my own in this regard, which I'm not embarrassed to tell you about, beloved partner: the first existential priority must be to find and respect the Truth, then it should be the love between couples, because a true couple is simply a mutating and perfect being in two bodies, then love for the best of our friends, including the relatives who deserve it, then would come our progress, our works and honouring our masters (you, for example), then would come care for everything that is valuable, wherever it is, you before anyone else, and only in the end would come in terms of priorities procuring the means for a dignified life, since that would be a mere consequence of a good scale of internal priorities.

And I allow you to correct me and to complete my programme, since I can't think of any more essential things.

- The Earth: Wow! I think your programme is a stroke of genius! I have no corrections and in respect of completing, all I can think of, from my age-old memory, is to include the recovery of those elevated creators of the past, offering them a place in your collective memory, and dispensing with all the middle-men who have interpreted their works as it suited them, what do you say?

- The People: I say it's a delight, a privilege and an honour, partner. For sure!

AND I DEMAND PASSIONATE SOLIDARITY!

- The People: The problem with today's salvaging love and solidarity is that it's merely a fashion, dear partner. Towards the end of the twentieth century, it became fashionable to be a cynical, competitive and predatory yuppie. Now, everyone speaks of love, solidarity, voluntary networks and NGOs. Meanwhile living on the margins of official society and peacefully coexisting with the major causers of the crisis. For now we can only speak, where love between human beings is concerned, of a cyclical fashion trend. And worst of all, precisely because it is a fashion, is the fact that playing Little Red Riding Hood, in ecstasy when faced with the wolf, mistaking him for the innocent and beloved grandma, is also fashionable. It's the in-thing to be naive, salvaging, and messianic too, I fear. Most probably, civil society is currently tempted to rescue this civilisation and to return it once more, restored, to the same people (perhaps wearing different masks) who finished it off.

So I believe that here, more than with any other subject, it's not redundant to start by defining concepts regarding that almost miraculous feeling, capable of working wonders and moving mountains when love is real, authentic: but which becomes a Stockholm syndrome and a threat for the sacrifice of the purest and most naive when love, as is the case today, is a social mannerism, an expression of what is politically correct, an anaesthetic that we could inject in ourselves to allow others to plunge the dagger in further.

I, as an already evolved – or at least evolving - People must denounce and protest against those pleas that confuse love and compassion. Compassion is beautiful, but it depends on sadness, on pain for the other's suffering, on the will to find solutions to problems and to take part in those solutions. Love has more to do with passion, with commitment towards the best in the other from the best in oneself. I cannot fall in love with the dark, diseased, disoriented parts of myself or of others. I can feel sorry for them if they're not harmful enough to threaten my own or others' integrity – because in that case I ought to fear them – but I can't love them. I can love what is loveable and feel very sorry if it has a cancer, but I can't and shouldn't fall in love with its cancer. Nor mine.

Going back to the sequence which I defend as being biologically mine and ours, the only valid base for love is worth, admiration for what is marvellous in others and in oneself, for what is advanced and attractive. We ought to decontaminate ourselves from those clichés of ecclesiastical origin that only serve to create feelings of guilt towards those who damage and punish us – adding it's for our own good! – and indifference towards what is truly loveable and committed – which they show us as being mere normality. Read banality, because if love, which is the most marvellous wonder is seen as banal, what **is** interesting, "mysterious", read addictively fascinating would then be evil, right? And therein lies the root of the great danger we're in now, of being "hooked" on the pseudo "mission" to redeem the bad guys, whom we don't even see as bad, but rather as "promises" of becoming prodigal sons. This is the greatest social danger at this moment, I warn you, partner, in case I'm circumstantially overcome in rapture to become a fashion victim.

Since we're defining love and its social expression, solidarity, I would say that it's something like the innate capacity to create for oneself and others a safe space where each can be or become what they were born to be. In other words, an internal and external space, cleanly shared, in which we can all not only preserve the little good that's left in us, but also recover the much that's marvellous that we've lost along the way. And all human beings have been born to be integrally free, happy and safe – and I mean being safe, not only to live in safety, but also to be safe and harmonious for others. And anything living in that same space, was also born to be free, happy and safe, whether these be animals, plants, seas, the atmosphere, the soil we plough or the ground we tread, in other words, you, beloved partner. You do know how to love without confusion, or guilt created to maintain stale and castrating authority.

And in social terms, the privileged areas of action where purified love and solidarity are concerned, would be, I believe, the family – including its protagonist: the couple -, drafting laws that protect society, the creation or maintenance of worthy guilds, associations that protect everything that is valuable and that promote a sense of belonging among their members, the union on an international level of groups of countries with shared and committed signs of identity – clearly not defensive or corporate oriented – the protection of socially and culturally valuable groups and races, considered to be World Heritage, protection programs for different age groups – for example, for that marvel that grandparents and the elderly represent – and for especially valuable activities – for example crafts and grandma's recipes, or of ethnic origin, for example the recovery of the spirituality of America's native Indians - or animals – such as protecting the blue whale.

I suppose that you've a lot to contribute on this subject regarding love and solidarity. And I would very much like to hear what you have to say.

- **The Earth:** It's a delight how you express yourself. You put into words what I've always felt through and through. I very much agree with your definition of love and with the areas of action that you point out. And it touches me deeply that you should believe that the foundation of love ought to be worth. Because, as we said when we spoke of sequences, my sequence starts with love and I give my love to everything that there is, because everything that there is, whether evolved or created, is valuable for me. But I only allow myself to be given and allow to prosper what is good, because if you sow in me something anti-natural I wouldn't even consider it a seed, and I'd never allow it to become a jungle that strangles its environment. I would simply ignore it, or better yet, I would choke it in me. From my billions of years in age, I've always loved all that is good that surrounded me and everything that inhabited me, and since very recently, little more than two million years, I've loved you more than anything else, because I felt that you were and you are, at least from what little I know of the Universe, the most evolved and complete thing that exists.

From my position as a planet, I see love as the only energy capable of sustaining the Universe. In fact, love is the only possible generator of negentropy. And without it, can you imagine that you could even exist? If chaos ruled the Universe, if there was no order, how could you exist as you are? And how could we be sharing this dialogue if at the same time we were bringing senseless chaos to each other, without rhyme or reason, subject to the greatest disorder? I can tell you one thing you might find exaggerated, but which isn't: without love, there would be no life, without love there would be nothing more than the most absolute nothingness.

And coming back to earth, without love, you wouldn't have intelligence, and without intelligence, you wouldn't be speaking to me, right?

So, we're on the wrong path if love is fashion and not art, as my dear Erich Fromm rightly saw... For you it must be Art; sublime art that stems from your pride. And art is what you are doing by conversing with me and by wanting to give yourself to everything that's good, to everything that's valuable, to everything that's marvellous in life.

When you start to feel doubts about love, talk to the sea, to my sea, which is yours. And be amazed at its movement and its colours, at its life and its force, generous and endless.

And coming back to the areas of action you proposed, I believe it's particularly relevant for you to relearn from your offspring, from your babies, true masters in the art of loving, and to protect and encourage that miracle that love is in them. I insist once again on basic education, but you see it doesn't make sense to unlearn to have to learn all over again. And moreover, I predict that this would help to greatly reduce the number of sociopaths among your members, since sociopathy is merely, although it may seem simplistic, the absence of love.

Do you find my vision of the subject correct, dear partner?

The People: With your permission, I quote: "It makes no sense to unlearn to have to learn all over again" How well you put it dear partner! And yes your vision – since eyes really are the sense of love and therefore the mirror of the soul – seems marvellous to me.

And yes, it's also true that babies ought to be the masters who teach us permanently that we're born perfect and that we don't have to do anything to be happy, except not to upset the natural order, not to "bring chaos" – as you say in such a striking manner – to what is perfect. And it's up to the family, to parents, to safeguard their children from over-adapting to resignation, to defeatism, not pushing them to sacrifice their talents and vocations through making them adapt to an inverted social sequence. Since unfortunately, the civilisation we've created still doesn't admire worth, doesn't admit exceptional talent, doesn't admit to being questioned by the pure and scrutinising gaze of the girl in the tale of The Emperor's New Clothes. Unfortunately, in this society, which we denounce and which we must assume as having built between all of us and which we must fix between all of us too, there's still no backing of the growth and blossoming of what's best in each and every one of us. We still prefer to project self-compassion onto others, and to love their most diseased and harmful parts with a clear conscience, without realising that in the end, we not only maintain the worst, but give it priority over the best, which we exhaust and sacrifice to the wolf of the moment. And that also outrages me.

But the good news is that we're in a generation of bridge-building and of alliances between grandparents and grandchildren, in which they encourage each other, the former with accumulated wisdom and the latter with the freshness and vitality of what's intact, of what hasn't yet been damaged. Therefore, parents, caught in that gentle grip, will be forced to choose to study and learn from their offspring and to respect the teachings of their own parents, illustrated by their grandchildren. In this sense, the wheel of love is already turning in the right direction.

Plus, going back to that fashion of saviour-NGOs, the positive aspect is that civil society has realised that it can replace Institutions and even work better than them. And that has allowed it to have the self-confidence to stand up and be heard and to take to the streets to demonstrate its outrage.

Another positive thing that we should applaud is the legitimising, the institutionalisation of love wherever it is and whoever it comes from. Nowadays adultery is no longer the cause for sanctions or blame in a divorce. Nowadays marriage between gays or lesbians has the same legitimacy and worth as between people with more traditional inclinations, nowadays the difference in age is no longer seen with horror if it's the man who's twenty years younger than the woman. Nowadays there's prison for abusing a child or a woman. And everything will be much more solid and truer once it's accepted with joy that a couple, that two people who love each other and who decide to stand up for their love together, have the highest and most important status in the scale of love. Much higher than the love between parents and children, or between blood brothers. Because a couple in love is the source of life, a blessing of eternal love for their children, brothers and sisters, friends, partners and parents. And also a social reference. This has yet to supersede existing social clichés.

Something else to be discovered and assumed, and applying our innate biological sequence, are THE AGES OF MAN (and woman, of course). Yes, each age also has its own dominant, non-deferrable and specific need. This revelation, partner, may surprise you, but I promise you that it's more than thought-through and based on the truth of life. To accept it and observe it is love in action. And I must warn you too that, for now, we do it in reverse. Take a look:

- During gestation, the foetus needs to feel the JOY of its mother and its surroundings, because a baby is a gift, a free token of the miracle of life. It's pure celebration. No other emotion is as indispensable for the safe development of a budding life.

- In early childhood, SAFETY is undeferrable for the infant: to know who he is, to see himself recognised and all his special talents encouraged, to be safe in the knowledge of who his parents are, where his roof is, what his schedule is, to acquire early knowledge of the boundaries nobody can breach against his integrity and that he must also respect to allow family life to flow in harmony. That is his indisputable existential thirst. This way he updates and reinforces the WHERE of things, and already knows from experience that the best of himself lies within himself, so he won't seek it or harm it in others.

  ❧ During late childhood and adolescence, the unquenchable existential thirst is for DEVELOPMENT, knowledge, thought, objective information, motivating communication, and also developing sensitivity and intelligence as much as possible so that the adolescent can increase his options, be less dependent, less symbiotic, have more autonomy. That way he will interiorise the WHAT of things, and will know how to relate and connect them in possible ways. He will no longer depend on others' charity and will know how to fend for himself objectively and never unrealistically.

  ❧ During early youth he needs, more than anything else, JUSTICE, to reject family and social rules and values, and establish his own, to choose who he wants to act out his leadership and cultural system with. That way he'll assume responsibility for his own current and future life, since nobody will have created it for him or imposed it on him. This way he'll come to know the HOW of things and will not allow himself to be manipulated or manipulate others. He will lay down values and build culture and will have interiorised already that he is social and fair, and that unanimity in consensus for what is good – i.e. healthy – is possible, and ceases to be a utopia.

🖋 During maturity, a human being is already prepared for CREATIVE TRANSFORMATION and to devote himself to his own work, starting by making his life his greatest work of art. That way he can leave a trail, and be not only useful but irreplaceable for himself and his surroundings. In this way he'll already know the WHY of things and will realise that one must go to the essence and dream imagining the quintessence of beauty, because what is beautiful is true and perfect.

🖋 In old age, his priority and preparation already allow him to achieve and preserve true BELONGING and there he'll realise that the love of a couple is the only thing that is irreplaceable, eternal, infinite and warm for him. And he'll extend that blissful and fulfilled love to the protection of his grandchildren and to the enjoyment of his friends, including his children. That way he will be a master of the WHEN of things and will know how to delight with what is essential already converted into permanence, sharing it with the best around him. He will be a home and a homecoming as well as a flame of hope for those around him.

🖎 In very old age, he will already be able to truly access PLENITUDE through true wisdom, spirituality and if he remained true and faithful to his nature, also to refinement and the exquisite nature of his sexual life with his partner. Yes, no joking. And to prepare himself for leaving this world with his partner TOGETHER AND AT THE SAME TIME, leaving an indelible wake of light. This way he will access the WHAT FOR of things, their FINALITY and will become a true Wise man for the enjoyment and gratitude of those who surround him.

But in real life, imposed as now, moving in the opposite direction to the most basic and essential biological needs of human beings, we see children educated with the illusion of impunity for all their whims, but under the Damocles' sword of "enjoy now child, you'll know what hard work is later on"; rebellious and castrated adolescents who become obsessed with urban gangs to flee from their family equivalents; young people full of arrogance who believe that youth is an eternal value envied by their elders and who become competitive predators; resentful and disillusioned adults who only find enjoyment in finding faults and culprits among the young as well as the old, their parents in particular who are blamed for all their chronic failures; sad old men, defeated, defeatists, tiresome and resigned who everyone wishes to abandon in an old folks' home with their equals; and feeble terrorised elders, since they managed to remain alone and ill from the time when they helped their weary spouses to die badly and have since become a mere dead weight for their dispersed families. Are you shocked by what I'm saying here, dear partner, you who preserve intact your grandmother, mother and baby, my now safe baby?

- **The Earth:** Well, dear People, I'm surprised but not shocked. I'm surprised at how novel it is and I'm surprised at how we've evolved during our conversations until managing to see with such clarity the natural, life loving, organic path that every human has inscribed in his being. I'm not shocked, because in Nature, among certain evolved animals and certain primitive peoples, a similar path occurs. You just have to observe the life of elephants or dolphins to find surprising parallels with your proposal.

Without forgetting that, in other times, reaching an advanced age was a sign of wisdom, not, like now, a bothersome family and social inconvenience: In Numbers, a book of the Old Testament, the creation of the Council of Elders appears as a divine initiative to help Moses, and in the cultures of ancient Greece and Rome, the Council of Elders results in what the Senate represents in modern democracies. That's why I insist on recovering the good things that you've already experienced as a People. And there are current encouraging initiatives in this regard, such as the creation in 2007 of the "The Global Elders" on the occasion of Nelson Mandela's 89th birthday.

And I'm outraged to think about the millions of human beings who've worked and continue to work in that perverse and unnatural sequence, fighting their whole life against the natural flow.

However, having found this out, we ought to move on from outrage to the joy of discovering a marvellous truth: the truth about the ages of man. And since we're at it, beloved partner, wouldn't it now be time to move onto this sixth and last dimension of what is human, that of Plenitude, that of truth and peace and joy, yours and mine?

- The People: You've already leaped ahead with your Council of Elders and placed yourself in that joy and that peace, which, for some reason, I guess mischievously, is precisely and "casually" your vocation. So I'm expectantly waiting, dear partner.

I'll finish by pointing out, since it would seem that we've not mentioned the Institutions that would guarantee that passionate solidarity that we're demanding, that the Legislative function in an evolved society, shouldn't be the object of political struggles but of caring and passionate consensus and it would be sufficient to have a dozen specialists in the drafting and enforcement of laws to prepare them. So I would suggest that said **Legislative Committee** works under a representative committee consisting of one representative of each body (Safety Council, Management Team, People's Chamber, College of Creators and two representatives from the Council of Elders, which we'll take a look at next). In this way, they'll receive proposals for laws that are genuinely functionally necessary and that stem from the bodies specialised in guaranteeing the care for my real motivations and needs. In the event of antagonism or poor communication, arbitration would be sought from the Council of Elders. That way society would have laws that truly protect me and you.

Another major problem: I don't recognise a Europe that consists only of the masculine half of the couple it ought to form organically. Europe is what exists today PLUS its feminine part, Russia, and all the countries that it annexed during Communism and beforehand too, during the Tsarist period. Masculine Europe is the creation of a marvellous Emperor, Charlemagne. And it also has its entire feminine side, which adores him and for which it is indispensable.

I wanted to leave those two things clear. Regarding international bodies of solidarity and consensus I believe that we ought to speak about them when we look at joy and peace, since unless their supreme objective and sole finality is peace, they're of no use to me.

Does this seem ok?

AND I DEMAND WISDOM IN TRUTH!

- **The Earth:** More than ok! And with no delay, let's move onto the sixth and last of universal human motivations: Plenitude.

And yes, it may be that this is "casually" my vocation.

I quote, from our conversations: "PLENITUDE: [...] in other words the cult of truth and peace, the only guarantors of the human being's and your vocation for happiness, in other words of the entire Universe, created and evolving."

I would say that the human being's vocation for happiness is not only a right, but also an obligation. And I would like before anything else, to denounce, outraged, the abundant sceptical, pessimistic, necrophiliac stances that say that being happy is for mental retards. A clear exponent of this barbarity is

Sigmund Freud, who once said "*there are two ways to be happy in this life, one is to play the fool and the other is to be one.*" If there are human beings for whom joy is forbidden, that's their problem – which they can manage to solve if they want - but please, don't contaminate the rest! Don't let them contaminate you, People!

And while we're at it, I'd also like to denounce relativists, who often share the stances of the former, and for whom truth doesn't exist, instead there are as many truths as there are human beings. This approach, which suggests that nothing is objective, that everything depends on your point of view, that everything is debatable and equally valid, and which taken to the extreme leads to the madness of not distinguishing what is real from what is imaginary, since nothing is real, is the human being's spiritual cancer. And I know what I'm talking about, since I'm full of relativists, relativists who adopted this concept in order to create war, famine, dictatorships, massacres and dreadful crimes against you, beloved partner. With the excuse of relativism, there are no Universal Human Rights, there is no Democracy, there's no Justice, there is NOTHING! Because nothing is true. And that's always an excuse for choosing one's own ego, in other words for playing with the other's heart and falling for the illusion – for that is what it is – of impunity and selfishness.

Well, truth exists, Universal Human Rights exist, Democracy exists, Justice exists. Things are improvable, and that is what we're dealing with in our conversations, but they exist and they are here and now – and he who denies it is either mad, or maddening. And improvability is, simply, getting closer to the truth.

And going back to plenitude, you, I, plants and animals, the Universe, are alive. And the mere fact of being alive is a cause for joyful celebration, isn't it?

Where are the obstacles to being happy? What prevents human beings from being happy? What can we do so that, naturally, all human beings can be entitled to joy? We have been spelling out the problems facing you and providing solutions. If we managed to eliminate our outrage by adopting those solutions could we be happy, you, beloved People, and I, the Earth?

- The People: Wow, dear partner! I believe I wasn't wrong in my diagnosis of your vocation for joy. And, now that I'm inspired and self-confident where proper diagnoses are concerned, I'm going to come out with something that may make you burst out in joyful laughter at this truth, or it may shock you, but here goes: I'm going to entrust you with the best-kept secret of this Universe we both passionately love. We don't have five senses, as scientists have convinced us to date, but six. The five traditional ones, and each one as an antenna that amplifies, receives and emits all the signals for satisfying one of those human needs and motivations that we've already examined, it's true: touch, related to safety and fear; hearing, the antenna of sensitivity to sadness, and the guarantor of development; smell, connected to rage and justice; taste, related to transformation and creative pride; sight, bound to the soul governed by love and belonging, yes, but the sixth and most important sense, connected to plenitude, to joy, and to truth, is sex. And I'm not at all surprised by your great wisdom, although you, as you well say, possess only half of the human dimensions. And my affirmation is based on the fact that you are making love 24 hours a day with your beloved sky, making it so that for you day turns into a night of fusion and understanding, and night becomes day of communion and more truthful union. No, I'm not joking. Those dark and maddening people you speak of, those people without certainties are just people without possible orgasms, because truth is LIGHT and the orgasm of our spirit. And not only does it exist, but only that exists. We are developing embryos, tripping clumsily, on the path – sometimes castrated - towards it.

And forgive me, dear partner, for what may seem to you like my mania for defining things. This is very much related to those madmen you told me about: unless we define things, we can reach false agreements postulating that we share the same definition of something, or arrive at avoidable misunderstandings. Joy, as I experience it, could be defined as the innate capacity to flow in peace and freedom to find truth and certainties. Because truth isn't sought, it is only found with love and passionate and thankful giving to what is valid and advanced. The more truth there is: the more joy. And the more joy, the more fusion with truth. Joy inevitably carries us like this, towards our path of certainties regarding our existential FINALITY.

And yes, its sense is sex. We could say that truth is erotic whereas that relativism you speak of is sensationalist, and false, in other words, pornographic, mechanical, and extinguishing of all joy, of any exciting encounter with finality – which I have given the name VOCATION. So let's forget about it. At the end of the day, that relativism is merely a projection of internal vacuity and confusion.

But yes we have to face a major truth, that nowadays, even the Outraged, submerged in finding culprits for what many still see as a crisis and not as the collapse of a civilisation, don't see or even relate yet: today the requiem is playing for all ideologies, and even more so for the mega-ideologies which have been the major obstacles and middle-men between heaven, your beloved, and me. I refer to religions. The end of religions has arrived, and not because they're the people's opiate, but because they're that very thing which, as adults, we no longer need, middle-men between free human spirituality and your beloved heaven.

That doesn't prevent and rather demands, that I passionately love, and I suppose you more – since their bones lie buried in your loving bosom and their lives in your inexhaustible memory – the six founders of monotheistic religions, those wise and exceptionally advanced beings, those transcendental and marvellous beings nobody understood in their time, mediatised by their churches, simplifying them and more often than not betraying their words, their lives and their messages and which in the end only divided human beings and continue to divide them, with the aggravation of doing so in their venerable names. I love Moses and I love Jesus, I love Mohammed and I love Buddha, I love Zoroaster and I love Mani, I love them dearly and passionately and I believe that the entire Universe adores them and made them immortal. But as advanced human beings, as wise masters of human spirituality, not as mandates of subjugation and automatic obedience delivered down from God's voice, because that would be a God that denied Creation and Evolution.

But, nowadays, human beings want freedom and happiness, in other words for their spirit to flow and to find truth in an intimate and personal way. At most, they're willing to listen to other people's testimony, but not necessarily either. Nobody authentic likes to make love in public, much less to talk about their sensations, nor, much less, to convince anyone about them, nor, much less, to seek promiscuous adepts to share them with. Spirituality is the high and private domain of each human being. And spirituality just like the truths it reveals, are seen in a more dazzling and simpler way the more it raises its flight and sees us from increasingly higher levels. That, I believe, is the first trend and truth of the future. Because joy refers to Infinity, and consequently governs the vision of the future also. What can be improved never ends, by definition. Truth neither.

That way and only that way can the human being transcend his localism and aspire to claim his true identity: that of being UNIVERSAL.

Speaking of truth, I have so many things to tell you, dear partner! I want to speak to you about wisdom and about the Council of Elders as the maximum institution of the bio-humanist civilisation we yearn for, I want to tell you about the necessary fusion and complementarity between men and women, each claiming the best of what befalls them to associate with the other, I want to tell you about the Children's Council, the only institution capable of overriding and calling the council of elders to attention, I want to tell you about the society of the future that I clearly glimpse. And about much more. Where shall we begin dear partner?

- **The Earth:** Gee whiz! and all manner of other interjections of amazement you can think of! You've hit the nail on the head again! I never imagined that you'd manage to glimpse, to capture, as a People, as a collective entity, your finality, your ultimate sense. And I think you know how happy I am! And how happy Heaven is, that heaven that you've almost always considered distant, unapproachable, where all your longings lived inaccessibly, which now, by art of truth, can descend to me and be here, with us!

And now yes, finally, we are two listening to you and supporting you, two in whom you will find your staunchest allies, two in one, Heaven and Earth, who are Nature and Life, permanent flowing and mirror of JOY for you.

- Heaven and Earth: Speak to us, dear People, since we'll be delighted to see grounded in you what has so often been forbidden. And we'll be delighted to see how that dimension considered magical, of "illuminates" or "gurus" becomes humanly normal and everyday. And, where shall we start? Well let's start wherever you want, we're all open.

- The People: I'll take this, dear Heaven, in a purely token manner: I'll take it in the literal sense, like that cosmos, that atmosphere I breathe, that breath which, out of love and constancy, can move mountains and oceans and bring light to new stars and galaxies! I prefer it that way. That's how it was always meant to be and to remain, in the silence of my inner truth that was further enlightened by your voice. And only that.

But since the two of you speak, I'll speak of something in your very image and likeness: of myself having reached a higher state of evolution in which two, men and women, are cohabiting – not always seeing each other as we should, nor giving ourselves to each other as we'd like - without knowing ourselves, and, consequently, not valuing our similarities nor giving thanks for our differences. We are identical, yes, in terms of rights and status and motivations and needs and also finalities, meaning that WE ARE ONLY ONE in two. Traditionally, it's true, insistence was made on our differences, and there are differences, thankfully, and I'm not just speaking about the physical aspect and sense of truth, sex. Females, as such, had to develop their motivations more and therefore to establish more neuronal connections towards safety, justice, corporality - to carry and feed their offspring - and belonging. Males also had, in that distribution of roles and work, to develop further their dimensions of development, creation and spirituality. That's how things are and I'll refrain from giving a long list of examples that would only aspire to open doors that have always been open.

But a real WOMAN, who raises herself to the dignity of being human, has known, permanently – while preserving her three most traditionally feminine dimensions – how to develop her dimensions of intelligence, creation and spirituality as her gender's existential passion. And a MAN worthy of this name has done the same with the vocational development of his supposedly feminine dimensions. He developed to the utmost his capacity for respect, justice and universal love. Now it's time they recognised each other as friends, partners, and vocational spouses and to share everything at the same level of commitment and retribution. The end of the gender war is here, the end of mythical opponents who threaten each other with proving to the other that he/she could live perfectly well and better off by designing – out of spite and disdain – a world amputated of its BEST half.

The fact that the third millennium could be, as it threatens to want to be, the millennium of woman, to compensate and even out five millennia dominated by man, would simply be a waste of time and energy. And of darkness of the spirit. And of disorientation for children, those wise beings who ought to rule our society and have the distinguished privilege of being consulted by that Council of Elders and even admonishing them if necessary.

THE COUNCIL OF ELDERS ought to be, without distinction of age, sex, nationality, creed or colour, the supreme body of each Nation. The difference between a wise person and a genius – although the Wise person may also be a genius – is that the wise person is more spiritual because he has accessed a higher level of TRUTH. Thus, the wise person transcends safety to transform it into harmony, transforms development into clarity, justice into corporality - because he listens to his body which leads him away from liars and bloodsuckers - transforms creation into evolving mutation, belonging into benevolence, and spirituality into the wisdom of certainties, filled with gratitude and with the desire never to be right, always wanting the other to be.

The selection of these wise people will be difficult because we'll have a lot of dinosaurs as candidates. But it's inevitable to make ourselves be governed by that institution with deep historical roots, and even more so in an age of bridges between grandparents and children. This council should not have any formal power, and would merely hold the right to issue admonishments and guideline recommendations, publicised, it should be said, by all media and by the official state gazette. Three admonishments from this supreme body would be equivalent to a moral veto to continue occupying an official post in any of the formerly proposed bodies. And two recommendations would guarantee that we were dealing with a wise person, even if he were an illiterate road sweeper.

And only the **National Children's Assembly** – since we're talking about children it's surplus to say that "national" is precisely to indicate that there's room to be ruled by all the colours, creeds and nationalities of each country – could criticise them. And that assembly would be elected in equal measure by the Safety Council, the College of Creators, and the Council of Elders. Election of the Council of Elders would be by recommendation and with the consensus of the College of Creators and the Safety Council, which would put forward their candidates to the People's Chamber and that choice must follow a single criteria: for each member of those institutions to ask themselves just one question: Would I love, when I'm older or in a dream life, to be like them, or even more, to have had those people as my grandparents? If they consult with the child that still sleeps and lives in them, they will know how to choose the best. Hopefully, at some time that Council of Elders would be made up of people such as Martin Luther King, Gandhi, Mandela, Gorbachev, or King Juan Carlos I!

On an international level, and even more so in an age when planetary virtual interrelation is instantaneous, only the **International College of Creators** and the **International Council of Elders** ought to govern relations between countries, because that way the People as such would exist and build their own civilisation, their BIO-CIVILISATION. And this is not utopia, it's just a good vision of the future, of the kind that finally opens the doors to infinity as the only safe place. The sooner we see it and join together to build it, the better off we'll be.

- **The Earth:** Dear partner, the future is yours! Rather, the future is ours!

Your ideas are brilliant and I presage that done that way, peace and joy will be a constant.

All that remains for me to do is to thank you for the trust you have given me in the course of our conversations and to congratulate you. To thank you for having wanted to listen to me, for treating me with the kindness and respect that I believe will be the keynote from now on, for making me feel that you love me and will do everything possible to take care of me and protect me, for teaching me so many things and making me see that your splendour may become the greatest splendour on me, and that I may grow and evolve hand in hand with you. I feel enormously privileged because you, with your six dimensions, have made me, with just three, a participant in your evolution. And along the way, I too have evolved by your side. Thanks to you, I will no longer succumb to indiscriminate love, false joy or false safety. You have made me see, and I am infinitely grateful for it, that for everything to flow in peace each individual must be on alert to make sure that their dimensions are balanced and fed with the right emotion.

And I would like to congratulate you, since I feel like the mother dazzled by her child, like the grandmother who sees her grandson triumph and whose eyes are filled with joy at seeing that her grandchild will have a safe and peaceful future. So don't be surprised if, as I tell you this, you feel rain on your skin. Don't worry; it's my tears of joy and gratitude.

Your initial outrage has progressed until reaching an ambitious, but realistic, pacific and natural vision of the future. As of now, you know you can count on me as a friend and as a partner forever.

So here, and now, we have our NOW WHAT!